Let's Celebrate Latino Holidays

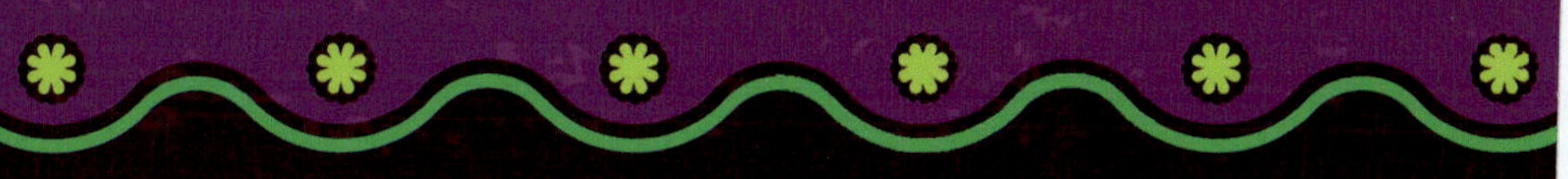

DAY OF THE DEAD

Sadie Silva

Please visit our website, www.enslow.com. For a free color catalog of all our high-quality books, call toll free 1-800-398-2504 or fax 1-877-980-4454.

Library of Congress Cataloging-in-Publication Data
Names: Silva, Sadie, author.
Title: Day of the dead / Sadie Silva.
Description: New York : Enslow Publishing, [2023] | Series: Let's Celebrate Latino Holidays | Includes index.
Identifiers: LCCN 2021037506 (print) | LCCN 2021037507 (ebook) | ISBN 9781978527249 (library binding) | ISBN 9781978527225 (paperback) | ISBN 9781978527232 (set) | ISBN 9781978527256 (ebook)
Subjects: LCSH: All Soul's Day–Juvenile literature. | Mexico–Social life and customs–Juvenile literature.
Classification: LCC GT4995.A4 S58 2023 (print) | LCC GT4995.A4 (ebook) | DDC 394.266–dc23
LC record available at https://lccn.loc.gov/2021037506
LC ebook record available at https://lccn.loc.gov/2021037507

First Edition

Portions of this work were originally authored by Marisa Orgullo and published as *Celebrating Day of the Dead!*. All new material this edition authored by Sadie Silva.

Published in 2023 by
Enslow Publishing
29 E. 21st Street
New York, NY 10010

Designer: Katelyn Reynolds
Interior Layout: Rachel Rising
Editor: Caitie McAneney

Photo credits: Cover, Dina Julayeva/Shutterstock.com; Cover, pp. 1-4, 6, 8, 10, 12, 14, 16, 18, 20, 22-24 (background) Cienpies Design/ Shutterstock.com; Cover, pp. 1, 3, 23, 24 (text box) scoutori/Shutterstock.com; Cover, pp. 1, 3, 23, 24 (text) Cienpies Design/Shutterstock.com; p. 5 Quetzalcoatl1/Shutterstock.com; p. 7 Benjamin Lopez G/Shutterstock.com; p. 9 Davide Palli/Shutterstock.com; p. 11 Marcos Castillo/ Shutterstock.com; p. 13 Belikova Oksana/Shutterstock.com; p. 15 Fer Gregory/Shutterstock.com; p. 17 Fer Gregory/Shutterstock.com; p. 19 Victor Baril/Shutterstock.com; p. 21 mark reinstein/Shutterstock.com; p. 22 ProStockStudio/Shutterstock.com.

Printed in the United States of America

Some of the images in this book illustrate individuals who are models. The depictions do not imply actual situations or events.

CPSIA compliance information: Batch #CSENS23: For further information contact Enslow Publishing, New York, New York, at 1-800-398-2504.

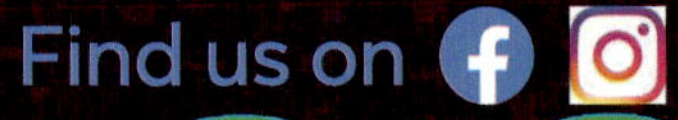

CONTENTS

Words in the glossary appear in **bold** type the first time they are used in the text.

A Time to Remember

It can be sad to think about your loved ones who have died. But some **Latino** people **celebrate** their lives on *Día de los Muertos*, or Day of the Dead. This holiday takes place on the first two days in November. Families get together to share food, music, and memories.

Día de los Muertos is a time to remember people who have died. Even children celebrate this holiday.

Day of the Dead is a special **tradition** in Latin American **cultures**, especially in Mexico. It goes back to early groups of people living in what is now Mexico, including the Aztecs. They believed the spirits of the dead traveled back to Earth once a year. They left the spirits offerings of flowers and fruit.

People believe leaving flowers and food will help the spirits of their loved ones in their journey.

Day of the Dead is a mix of early Mexican traditions and **Catholic** traditions. Many Catholics celebrate All Saints' Day on November 1 and All Souls' Day on November 2. Spanish Catholics came to Mexico in the 1500s. These days became a part of the tradition in Mexico.

Some Catholics go to church on All Saints' Day and All Souls' Day.

Making an Ofrenda

To remember loved ones, families set up an *ofrenda* (oh-FREN-duh) in their home or at a **grave**. An *ofrenda* is an **altar** with photos of the dead. Children write notes and draw pictures. Families gather around the *ofrenda* and think about happy memories.

Keeping a person's memory alive is important in Latino cultures.

People also place gifts on their *ofrendas*. They decorate with skulls, or **skeleton** heads, and rows of colorful paper cutouts called *papel picado* (pa-PEL pee-KAH-thoh). Bright marigold flowers welcome the spirits. Marigolds are laid out to guide the spirits to their families.

Skulls are common decorations for Day of the Dead.

Special Foods

Food is an important part of traditions. For Day of the Dead, families cook foods that their loved ones liked. They feast on **tamales** made with meat, cheese, or nuts. They snack on fruit and sweets. Some families pack up the feast and eat it by a loved one's grave.

Picnics in graveyards are common in Mexico on Day of the Dead.

People also eat a special bread called *pan de muerto* (PAHN DEH MWER-toh), or bread of the dead. Many bakers shape and decorate the bread. It has a round piece on top and thin strips on the sides to look like a skull and bones.

Pan de muerto is a yummy way to celebrate Day of the Dead.

Day of the Dead isn't supposed to be sad, though. People laugh and play! People dress up and wear makeup to look like skeletons. They take part in lively parades. Music is an important part of Day of the Dead. People sing and play instruments.

People dress up skeletons and place them to look like they're playing soccer, shopping, or driving.

Keeping Traditions Alive

Day of the Dead is celebrated in Latin America. But Latino people in the United States also celebrate this holiday. Mexican Americans build *ofrendas* and eat *pan de muerto*. Mexican Americans and other Latinos celebrate their family members who have died, even if they aren't close to their graves.

Los Angeles, California, is a city with many Latino people. They hold Day of the Dead celebrations.

Thinking about skeletons and graves might not seem joyful. However, Latino people find joy in celebrating the lives of their loved ones who have died. They take time to remember the people they once knew. Day of the Dead is a day to celebrate life!

GLOSSARY

altar A table or a stone on which offerings are made.

Catholic A member of the Roman Catholic faith.

celebrate To honor with special activities.

culture The beliefs and ways of life of a group of people.

grave A place where a dead person is buried.

Latino Someone who lives in Latin America or whose family is from Latin America.

skeleton The bones that give animals' or people's bodies shape.

tamale Cornmeal dough rolled with ground meat or beans and seasoning, wrapped in corn husks, and steamed.

tradition Something that has been done for a long time.

FOR MORE INFORMATION

Books

Greenfield Thong, Roseanne. *Día de Los Muertos.* New York, NY: Albert Whitman, 2020.

Morlock, Rachael. *The People and Culture of Mexico.* New York, NY: PowerKids Press, 2018.

Websites

Day of the Dead
kids.nationalgeographic.com/celebrations/article/day-of-the-dead
Explore the origins and celebrations of Day of the Day with National Geographic Kids.

Five Facts about Día de Los Muertos (Day of the Dead)
www.si.edu/stories/5-facts-about-dia-de-los-muertos-day-dead
Read some fun facts about Day of the Dead from Smithsonian.

Publisher's note to educators and parents: Our editors have carefully reviewed these websites to ensure that they are suitable for students. Many websites change frequently, however, and we cannot guarantee that a site's future contents will continue to meet our high standards of quality and educational value. Be advised that students should be closely supervised whenever they access the internet.

INDEX